YES...
The Old Testament CAN Make Sense to You

KENT ADRIAN

YES...
The Old Testament CAN Make Sense to You

The Three Storylines That Will Help You Understand What God Wants You to Hear in the Old Testament

XULON PRESS

Xulon Press
2301 Lucien Way #415
Maitland, FL 32751
407.339.4217
www.xulonpress.com

© 2019 by Kent Adrian

Unless otherwise indicated, Scripture quotations taken from the Holy Bible, New International Version (NIV). Copyright © 1973, 1978, 1984, 2011 by Biblica, Inc.™. Used by permission. All rights reserved.

Printed in the United States of America.

ISBN-13: 978-1-5456-7276-1

Life Impact Connections, Inc.

"Rediscovering the Genuine Gospel and Its Amazing Impact on Life"

www.lifeimpactconnections.org

—Table of Contents—

Study guide questions are available by going to lifeimpactconnections.org.

(Books/Study Guides panel)

On this website, you will also find additional tools to help nurture an understanding of the genuine gospel and how that gospel promotes a spiritual and emotional health that responds to life with strength and confidence.

—*Acknowledgments*—

I am grateful for the willingness and time of both Pauline (Peen) Hardy and Sarah Baker in reviewing this book and their helpful editing suggestions. I view myself as more of a communicator of Christian truth than I do a writer, so their involvement with me in producing *YES... The Old Testament CAN Make Sense to You* has been invaluable.

It is difficult to write major sections of a book in the middle of day-to-day responsibilities and distractions. My ability to have a place that provided the chance to focus on writing was due to the gracious generosity of Henry and Ellen Kane as well as Nancy Kerley. Allowing me to use their condos, with tranquil views of the ocean and a quiet space, is much appreciated.

—PART ONE—

—1—

AN ADMISSION

L et's just admit it from the start—the Old Testament can be really difficult to wade through.

For one thing, it's long. The Old Testament is comprised of thirty-nine separate books (some are short, but most are fairly long), and it makes up two-thirds of the entire Bible. No matter how much you already know or don't know about the Bible, the Old Testament takes a long time to read.

In addition, there are substantial parts that, to be honest, are not always very captivating. There are some rather extensive genealogies I doubt a whole lot of people have actually made it through. You can read "who begat whom" only so many times before you simply give up on reading them. The genealogies have some important things to say, but we aren't going to discover their insights without some help from those who study such passages. The genealogies certainly are not where most people go for devotional inspiration. Then there are all those laws. A whole book (Leviticus) is basically a recitation of laws and details about a sacrificial system that, on the surface, doesn't seem to be relevant to us today. Most people who try to read the Bible from cover to cover give up somewhere in the book of Leviticus.

Perhaps the single greatest reason the Old Testament is difficult to read, however, is that it contains many historical references to which readers today have no connection. We have no idea why certain events, people, or places may or may not be significant for us. For example, in the book of Jonah, God calls Jonah to go and preach about God's love and mercy to the people of

Nineveh. Jonah refuses and ends up being swallowed by a great fish. Anyone reading the story will pick up on the idea Jonah doesn't want to do what God commands, so he runs away. But it adds a lot of power and drama to the whole story if you understand that Jonah wasn't just running to the next town. Jonah ran to Tarshish, a town more than 2,500 miles from Israel and 180 degrees in the opposite direction from Nineveh. Tarshish was a remote town located on the western coast of what is today Spain. Jonah couldn't go any farther. He was running as far as he could possibly get from where God wanted him to go.

It also helps to know that Nineveh wasn't just any pagan city. The people of Nineveh were a cruel and wicked people. As Timothy Keller notes in his book *The Prodigal Prophet*:

> *Assyria was one of the cruelest and most violent empires of ancient times. Assyrian kings*

often recorded the results of their military victories, gloating of whole plains littered with corpses and of cities burned completely to the ground. The emperor Shalmaneser III is well known for depicting torture, dismembering, and decapitations of enemies in grisly detail on large stone relief panels. Assyrian history is "as gory and blood-curdling a history as we know." After capturing enemies, the Assyrians would typically cut off their legs and one arm, leaving the other arm and hand so they could shake the victim's hand in mockery as he was dying. They forced friends and family members to parade with the decapitated heads of their loved ones elevated on poles. They pulled out prisoners' tongues and stretched their bodies with ropes so they could be flayed alive and their skins displayed on city walls. They burned adolescents alive. Those who survived the destruction of their cities were fated to endure cruel and violent forms of slavery. The Assyrians have been called a "terrorist state."[1]

We can get the main point of the story of Jonah without knowing all of the details, but these facts do add to our understanding in a significant way. Jonah was afraid if he told the Ninevites of God's mercy that they would repent, and Jonah passionately didn't want that to happen. Jonah wanted to see God's justice for the Ninevites, not His mercy.

Jonah is a short story that is easy to read, and we can grasp the idea of its message even though we don't understand all the references. However, when a lot of the Old Testament is dealing with people like the Amorites, the Hittites, the Amalekites, and all the other "ites," reading it can seem to us like an irrelevant history lesson. Therefore, many Christians simply stay away from reading the Old Testament, and in doing so, they miss out on some very important insights into the character and purpose of God.

This book, *YES... the Old Testament CAN Make Sense to You*, is meant to help you read the Old Testament in a way you will find personally meaningful and significant. This current book is meant as a companion to my earlier work, *HELP... I Want to Read the Bible but I Don't Know How*, a book which focuses primarily on the New Testament. Because the three keys and the three questions found in *HELP...* are also very relevant to the Old Testament, I would recommend reading that book as well. *YES...the Old Testament CAN Make Sense to You* can be read on its own, but by reading both books and applying the lessons of each to the Old and New Testaments, you will have a much fuller understanding of how it is possible to read the Bible without having a lot of biblical background and still hear God's primary message.

God doesn't change. The God of the New Testament is the same God of the Old Testament. This one, unchanging God has a message for you about who He is and what His purpose is all about. That message is certainly given in the New Testament in its fullness, but the message begins in the Old Testament—and it's a message you can understand. The key is found in three storylines.

—2—

STORYLINES

The facts are quite incredible when you stop to think about them: the Bible is comprised of sixty-six separate books, written by some forty authors over approximately 1,600 years, and yet it has essentially a *singular* story. How can that possibly be? You couldn't take sixty-six separate works by forty different authors living in very different time periods anywhere in the history of literature and have them tell a singular story involving a common, unified plot. How can this be true about the Bible?

The answer to that question is very simple. Behind the writings of these sixty-six books stands a single author—God. II Timothy 3:16 is making precisely this point that God is the one who is behind what is communicated in the Bible when it says, "All Scripture is God-breathed..." God is telling us His story over time, in various cultures, through all manner of events involving diverse people, but it is still *His* story involving *His* purpose. That story can be summed up like this:

> **Because of His great love for us, God is taking what has become broken and is making all things new—and the key to making everything new is His work through Christ's death and resurrection, which makes it possible for us to be restored to our relationship with Him as our God.**

The story of the Bible is a rescue-and-restore story. People often say the Bible is a love story—and it is—because what God is doing in the

Bible is motivated by His love for us. However, this love story of God is primarily about a rescue-and-restore mission. And because the Old Testament is a major part of this singular story of rescue and restoration by God, we can better understand His message if we are aware of some simple storylines that run throughout its pages.

Storylines are crucial to understanding why events are taking place and what makes them important. For example, if I have been caught up in watching a particular detective series on TV, and my wife, who has never seen a single episode of this series, sits down to watch with me, at some point she is certain to say, "What's going on?" Now I have a choice: either I can say, "Too much has happened for me to explain"—in which case she will remain confused and lose interest—or I can give her some major storylines that will provide insight. Storylines will give her, in a brief, concise manner, the framework as to why something is taking place. If she understands the major storylines, she can fit in the details taking place on her own. Without understanding the major storylines, she is likely to be lost until she watches enough episodes to piece together the major storylines for herself. In any case, she needs the storylines to make sense of the details.

In a short, simple account, how would you describe the major storylines to someone who has never seen a single movie of the block-buster series *Star Wars*, or *Harry Potter*, or *The Avengers*, or whatever your favorite TV series or movie is? Try it. If you do a good job of telling the major storylines, a new viewer may be con-fused in spots, but even if you aren't around to give more information, that person can still make sense of what is happening and why the charac-ters are behaving the way they are.

Three storylines are essential to make sense of the Old Testament. If you recognize and iden-tify these three storylines, you will grow in your understanding of God's message for you. If you don't understand these key storylines of the Old Testament, you may have all kinds of knowledge about the Old Testament, and even about the Bible as a whole, but you will be missing out on God's primary message.

To be sure, there are storylines in the Old Testament other than these three, but my point is that the three I am about to give make up the central message of the Old Testament—and the additional storylines we could say are, in fact, related to these three primary storylines in some way as well.

Here are the three storylines that run throughout all of the Old Testament:

1. **The brokenness of God's good creation**
2. **God's reaction to that brokenness**
3. **God's promise about the brokenness**

These three storylines are on display in the Old Testament in major ways.

As you read the Old Testament, remember God has a plan and a purpose He is accomplishing. He is the one who is directing history in fulfillment of that plan; history is not the happening of random events. As is often said, Christianity is about who He is and what He has done, not who we are and what we need to do. It is in the Old Testament where that story of who He is and what He has done begins.

—3—

LIFE IS BROKEN

Genesis 1 teaches us something very important: God created everything, and what He created was good. In fact, God declares His creation not just "good," but "very good" (Gen. 1:31).

Life was experienced by the first human beings (Adam and Eve) as satisfying, joyful, and enriching. Adam and Eve enjoyed their relationship with God, they enjoyed their relationship with each other, and they enjoyed their work in God's creation where everything was an incredible expression of the majesty and goodness of God. Life was wonderful. Don't skip over this point; it is quite important to remember how God originally meant for things to work.

Then something went terribly wrong. Rather than live in this relationship with their Creator as their God—that is, as the one around whom lives revolve and for whom humanity was created—Adam and Eve decided they wanted to make life about themselves. This desire to be in charge is what the serpent referred to in Genesis 3:4 when he said to Adam and Eve, "You will not certainly die…For God knows that when you eat from it your eyes will be opened, and you will be like God, knowing good and evil." Ever since that time, we have wanted to make life about us rather than letting our lives revolve around God. It was because of this rejection of God as our God that everything in God's creation became broken. When we live apart from the God for whom we were created, life doesn't work as He designed it to work. It's not just that we as people became broken—all of creation felt the effects of this fall. The results were devastating; nothing now works as God intended for it to work.

Here is the point you need to remember: *One of the major purposes of the Old Testament is to describe the brokenness of life and the seriousness of this brokenness.* This point is very different from seeing the purpose of the Old Testament as giving us rules and standards by which we are expected to live and simply exhorting us to try harder to follow them. If the purpose of the Old Testament is to encourage us to live better lives, it has failed miserably. If, however, a primary purpose of the Old Testament is to describe the brokenness sin has caused and the results of sin, then it does a spectacularly great job.

We see pictures of the brokenness that permeates life throughout the Old Testament:

- jealousy
- anger
- pride
- family discord
- relational difficulties and divisions

- dysfunctional attitudes
- murder
- a lust for power
- hearts driven by greed
- the desire to control, deceive, and manipulate
- death and disease
- famine
- wars
- despair
- fear
- worry
- an inability to trust in God

Many more examples could be listed. Brokenness is seen on nearly every page of the Old Testament, in nearly every relationship, in nearly every person. God is saying something to us about the way we now function and about the way life now works. The examples and events in the Old Testament are often given to us to make sure we don't miss an even greater point—*we don't need to try harder to live better; we need to be set free. We need to be set free from the sin that imprisons us and binds us to the downward pull of our self-oriented hearts.*

Life is broken. When you read the stories of the Old Testament, this brokenness and its disastrous consequences are on constant, vivid display. From this very important, central lesson the Old Testament is almost shouting out to us, we can make several key observations about life:

1. Because nothing works as it should, we shouldn't expect life to be easy or fair.
2. God is not to blame for the brokenness and tragedies we experience in this world. Rather, what He intended for us was "very good."
3. There is something about brokenness as we experience it that is tied to the breakage of our relationship with God.

4. We were created for something more than
    what we experience in this fallen world,
    and the brokenness points us toward that
    "something more." We feel instinctively
    in our hearts that something isn't right
    with what we see and experience. We
    rightly feel, "This isn't the way things
    are supposed to be."

If you let the Old Testament's dramatic
descriptions of brokenness lead you to reflect
on life in general and on your life in particular,
and if this reflection brings you to attitudes and
actions such as confession, repentance, grate-
fulness, worship, compassion, humility, joy,
and trust—then reading the Old Testament can
become a great blessing to you. If you connect
what you read to your life and allow the words
and stories to bring you into God's presence,
then you will be reading the Old Testament in
the way I believe the Bible is meant to be read.

———————————

On Sunday, November 5, 2017, a twenty-six-year-old man wearing tactical-type gear and a ballistic vest entered the First Baptist Church in the small town of Sutherland Springs, Texas, saying, "You all die." His intent was to kill everyone. In the end, twenty-six were dead and about twenty others were wounded. He methodically shot people in the head. Of those who died, ten were women, seven were men, and eight were children. One of those who died was the unborn baby of a woman who also died. I heard a radio report saying that among the victims were a young mother and her child whom she had fallen on top of in order to protect—without success. I listened to the continuing reports that week about the shooting as newsmen recounted what had happened. Almost every time I listened, I found myself with tears in my eyes.

The world is broken. We see the tragedies resulting from this brokenness all around us. Sometimes the grief the brokenness brings is almost too much to bear. When I see or hear of such brokenness, it makes my heart cry out, "Come soon, Lord Jesus." We weren't made for this brokenness. God, I believe, cries too at what has happened to His world. Jesus cried at the pain the death of His friend Lazarus caused others. He cried even knowing that He was going to raise Lazarus to life. The world is broken. Yes, I am sure that God cries over the brokenness that has entered His world.

4

GOD'S RESPONSE
OF JUSTICE

T he second major storyline of the Old Testament is God's response to what has happened because of the fall of mankind—His reaction to the brokenness.

In dealing with this second storyline, you will discover the answer to some of the most difficult questions people have about the Old Testament. People struggle with many of the events that occur in the Old Testament, and there is an answer to the questions those struggles produce. However, I want to warn you in advance, you probably won't always find the answer to be emotionally satisfying. The fact that the answer doesn't satisfy you doesn't mean it is wrong; it simply means there are going to be happenings in the Bible that you most likely will always struggle with a little bit. My own view on this problem is that I don't think it is quite fair for us to "judge God" (terrible phrase!) on this side of eternity. As I said in my book *BEDROCK*, my bedrock beliefs are that God is sovereign, He is good, and He loves me. I am going to rest in those convictions and allow what bothers me a bit to be dealt with when I can see and understand more clearly — on the other side of eternity.

God's response to brokenness is justice. Consequently, in the Old Testament justice is a dominant theme and, in many ways, might be considered *the* dominant theme. God is a just God. He must act justly; it is His character. Even as God is love and cannot do what is unloving and as He is good and cannot do what is not good, He is also just and cannot do what is unjust.

The Old Testament points to God's justice over and over:

In Genesis 18, Abraham pleads with God not to totally destroy the city of Sodom for its wickedness. In his plea, Abraham points to God's character of justice:

> *Then Abraham approached him and said: "Will you sweep away the righteous with the wicked? What if there are fifty righteous people in the city? Will you really sweep it away and not spare the place for the sake of the fifty righteous people in it? Far be it from you to do such a thing—to kill the righteous with the wicked, treating the righteous and the wicked alike. Far be it from you! Will not the Judge of all the earth do right?"* (Gen. 18:23-25)

In Deuteronomy 32, Moses proclaims the just character of God:

> *I will proclaim the name of the Lord,*
> *Oh, praise the greatness of our God!*
> *He is the Rock, his works are perfect,*
> *And all his ways are just,*
> *A faithful God who does no wrong,*
> *Upright and just is he.* (Deut. 32:3-4)

There are what we might consider positive and negative sides to justice.

The Positive:

In a broken world, where nothing works fully as it should, life is replete with acts and powers of injustice. This brokenness of life is why you see the God of justice calling for His people to act justly toward others. This call for justice is not a minor concern of God's—it is a *major* concern. In fact, the Old Testament is quite clear as to what God thinks about religious activity and beliefs that don't lead us to act toward others with care, fairness, and dignity. God gives it to us pretty straight in the following passage from Amos:

I hate, I despise your religious festivals;
your assemblies are a stench to me.
Even though you bring me burnt offerings and
grain offerings,
I will not accept them.
Though you bring choice fellowship offerings,
I will have no regard for them.
Away with the noise of your songs!
I will not listen to the music of your harps.
But let justice roll on like a river,
righteousness like a never-failing stream!
(Amos 5:21-24)

God's feelings can't be stated more clearly than that. Religious faith that doesn't reorient our hearts so that we care about what God cares about and hate what God hates isn't real faith.

26

And what God cares about is that we act justly toward others.

What does it mean to act with justice? The Hebrew word for justice is *mishpat*. As Timothy Keller notes in his book *Generous Justice*, *mishpat* is a word that emphasizes our action. It is a word that essentially has to do with treating people equitably and giving people their rights. Therefore, as Keller notes, justice is about "giving people what they are due, whether punishment or protection or care."[2]

Only God acts with perfect justice, for only God knows all that is involved in any given situation. But, as God's people, we are called to reflect God's concern for justice in the world. Justice is a characteristic that has to do with what is right on the basis of what one is due as a creation of God. Therefore, justice includes correcting abuses, being generous to others, and conducting relationships (with individuals and community) with fairness and equity.

Because all human beings are created in the image of God and have inherent God-given dignity and value, they are to be treated with dignity and value. Therefore, we are acting justly when we clothe those who have no clothes, feed the hungry, provide for those in need, welcome strangers, take care of orphans and widows, refrain from gossip, and treat the poor the same as the rich. You get the idea. We are acting justly when we treat *all* people in our world as being precious, equal, and greatly valued.

A lot of the Old Testament is calling us to act justly in this broken, self-oriented world; look for the ways this is done when you read it.

The Negative:

There is also a negative side to justice. Justice is responding to others based on what they are due. To be just, therefore, means to hold people appropriately accountable. The wrong that is in us and in the world must be dealt with as it deserves. God doesn't wink and say, "Oh, that's ok," to the wrong, evil, and sin in the world. He is a just God. He acts, and must act, justly. The evil, wrong, and sin which have so greatly defaced and twisted God's good creation and caused incalculable suffering deserve to be eliminated from the world that God created in order to reflect His love, goodness, and beauty.

Consequently, God must judge what is wrong. He must judge the wrong that is in the world, and He must judge the wrong that is in us. And the Old Testament makes it very clear that He *is* going to judge the world and all that is wrong in it. If He didn't do this, He wouldn't be a just or good God. If you want to think about something really scary, think about what it would mean to have an all-powerful being who wasn't concerned with what is good or right.

God's judgment isn't the capricious, arbitrary anger caused by having His feelings hurt. God's judgment is the only reaction He can have to what is wrong. He must, and will, judge the sin and evil that have so imprisoned His creation.

In C. S. Lewis's *The Chronicles of Narnia* series, Lewis captures some of this truth in the book *The Lion, the Witch, and the Wardrobe*. Aslan, the great lion who is the Christ figure in this fantasy telling of the Christian story, hasn't been in his land of Narnia for a very long time. However, there are prophecies about his eventual return. One such prophecy speaks of his judgment on what is wrong and the new life that will be restored:

Wrong will be right, when Aslan comes in sight;
At the sound of his roar, sorrows will be no more;
When he bares his teeth, winter meets its death;
And when he shakes his mane, we shall have spring again.[3]

We are living under a curse, but the curse is going to be judged by the God of justice and goodness. The curse isn't going to have the final word.

We can now understand why judgment is such a strong theme in the Old Testament. God is a God of justice. Life and people are going to be dealt with as they deserve. So, yes, when the wickedness of humanity reaches certain points, God foreshadows the ultimate future judgment everyone will one day face by allowing forces to destroy the people or drive them out from what was the promised land.

The clear message of the Old Testament is that sin and evil are not going to win. They will be judged and eliminated from God's creation. So you have the people of Noah's day being wiped out by the flood, and the people living in the land that is to be given to Israel being conquered, killed, and driven out. However, it is important to note the people are not conquered, killed, or driven out until their wickedness has escalated to a certain point. In Genesis 15:16, we read where God speaks to Abraham concerning the promised land: *"In the fourth generation your descendants will come back here, for the sin of the Amorites has not yet reached its full measure."* God's judgment is always a just judgment.

The Old Testament tells us about God's just character in regard to our sinfulness:

- God's judgment and justice are the reason the whole **sacrificial system** of the Jewish people had to be instituted.
- The justice of God is displayed in the **building of the temple** where God's presence symbolically resided in the Holy of Holies, which is separated from sinful humanity.
- The justice of God is experienced in the **life of Israel** when, because of their

continued unfaithfulness, they are conquered by other countries and taken
into exile.

The major theme of the justice of God in the
Old Testament, in both its positive and negative
aspects, cannot be overstated. As previously
mentioned, it is a fair assessment to say that *this
is the dominant theme of the Old Testament*: the
sinfulness of humanity resulted in the brokenness of all people, and all life and must be met
with justice. In the case of dealing with what is
wrong, that means judgment.

I once took a religion class on the New
Testament at a secular university. I remember the
professor saying to the class, "My God is the
God of the New Testament, not the God of the
Old Testament." He went on to say, "The God of
the New Testament is loving, gracious, and mer-
ciful. The God of the Old Testament is vengeful,
angry, and full of wrath." This perspective on

the different testaments might seem reasonable
to someone who picks up the Old Testament and
doesn't understand that the judgment of God that
is so prevalent in the Old Testament is only part
of a larger story—a rescue story.

The God of the Old Testament is the same
God as the God of the New Testament. It is
simply that the purpose of the Old Testament is
to show us how great our need is, as those who
are sinful, in light of who God is. We deserve
judgment. Therefore, God can do nothing other
than judge what is wrong—and He will. If that
were the end of the story, it would be a very dark
and tragic story. However, it is not the end; it
isn't even the main purpose of the story, though
in the Old Testament it might seem that way.

Is God going to destroy everything and
everyone as if they never existed? No! He is going
to rescue His creation, and part of the Old Testament
points us to that rescue. God's light and love and

grace break forth with all of their brilliance in the New Testament, but they peek through the dark clouds of the Old Testament as well. Throughout the pages of the Old Testament, we see clues of God's promise concerning brokenness.

As I type these words, there is a story in the news about a fourteen-year-old girl who was raped in the bathroom of her school. The evidence that it was in fact a rape rather than a consensual act appears quite strong. Yet the authorities involved decided not to do anything about it because of who the accused happened to be. How does that make you feel? Assuming the facts are true as I just presented them, that story should make you upset, angry, and bothered. Why? Because you know that justice wasn't done. It isn't good or right when wrongdoing is not dealt with as wrong but is simply dismissed or ignored. If that quality is true for us as finite, sinful people, how much more must it be true of a holy, good, and just God? The evil and wrong that has entered this world will be dealt with by our Creator. It must be. Justice demands it. Our God is a just God. The Old Testament couldn't make this point any clearer.

5

GOD'S PROMISE OF RESTORATION

T he first chapter of this book gives several reasons why the Old Testament can be difficult: it takes a long time to read, it sometimes seems irrelevant, and the references are often foreign to us. There is another reason we have a difficult time with the Old Testament—it comes across very negatively.

The Old Testament is, in many ways, a very dark book. There is a reason for that darkness. The darkness is there because God is trying to get us to see something about ourselves, about Him, and about life. However, the awareness He first has to awaken us to is that the situation we are in isn't good. All of life, including humanity, is under a curse. This curse has defaced and distorted the way He made us. In addition, we have no ability to do anything about our condition. We can't change things by trying harder, being nicer, doing the best we can, or becoming religious. As Isaiah 64:6 declares, *"All of us have become like one who is unclean, and all our righteous acts are like filthy rags..."* This is the message the Old Testament wants to get across to us. When you understand the situation as God paints it in the Old Testament, it is very dark indeed!

However, that description is not the main story that is being told; it is only the prelude to the main story. The main story, even though it is not the part that receives the most attention, is God's promise concerning brokenness. This promise of God is an incredible one—He isn't going to let the brokenness win! He is going to rescue and restore what has been broken.

You will never understand the Old Testament until you understand this: *the purpose of the Old Testament is to prepare us for, and to point us to, the promise of God's rescue mission.* When you read the Old Testament, this rescue and restore purpose must always be in the background of your thinking, no matter the particular passage you may be reading.

The Old Testament is not producing a set of rules for you to live by. We are indeed to live out God's laws, both outwardly in action and inwardly in attitude, but the message of the Old Testament is that we constantly fail to follow them. Thus, the rules function to show us how far short we fall from what God made us for. This concept is what Romans 5:20 points to when it says, *"The law was brought in so that the trespass might increase. But where sin increased, grace increased all the more."* Galatians 3:24 says, *"So the law was our guardian until Christ came that we might be justified by faith."* The law's effect is to highlight our need.

The Old Testament characters are not, usually, examples given for you to model, the exception being Daniel. The purpose of the whole book of Daniel is to encourage faithfulness in the midst of a society that has no desire to live for God. All the other "heroes" of the Bible are deeply flawed people. Rather than hearing the message, "This is how I want you to live; follow this person here," we should be reading in amazement about the God who has chosen to use deeply flawed people in the carrying out of His incredible plan.

And God's message in the Old Testament repeatedly is, "I want you to know that My plan of rescue and restoration is going to be accomplished by My power and grace alone, not by anything that is super nifty about you!" For example:

- It isn't the older brother with the rightful birthright, Esau, that God chooses to carry out the family line for the plan of His redemption, but the younger brother, Jacob, who is quite the scoundrel (Gen. 25:24-34).

- Before Gideon can go to battle, his army must be cut down in size from twenty-two thousand to three hundred. Only then does God give permission for them to fight against the enemy, the Midianites (Judg. 7:1-8).

- When God chooses Israel's second king, David, all of David's older brothers are passed over. A young boy whom no one has thought of as special is chosen.

- The prophecy of the promised Messiah through whom God would rescue His people was to come from the most insignificant tribe of Israel, Judah (1 Sam. 16:1-13).

Do you feel that you are a broken, flawed, insignificant person? Perfect! Those are the ones who God uses most in His plan when they give their hearts to Him to be used for His purposes. God is making absolutely sure that we get this picture. His story has to do with who He is and what He has done, not who we are or what we need to do. It is a story of His grace, not our strength, achievements, or goodness.

Examples in the Old Testament:

God's promise of rescue and restoration is scattered everywhere throughout the Old Testament. You won't understand the other storylines very well if you don't keep in mind that those other storylines are meant to lead us to His promise about repairing the brokenness.

- The promise is seen in the fall of humanity, when God tells Satan of the one He will send to destroy him: *"And I will put enmity between you and the*

woman, and between your offspring and
hers; he will crush your head, and you
will strike his heel" (Gen. 3:15).

• The promise is seen in the Israelites' being
  delivered from slavery out of Egypt:
  *"Therefore, say to the Israelites: 'I am
  the LORD, and I will bring you out from
  under the yoke of the Egyptians. I will
  free you from being slaves to them, and
  I will redeem you with an outstretched
  arm and with mighty acts of judgments'"*
  (Exod. 6:6).

• The promise is seen in the saving of the
  Israelites from death by the blood of a
  sacrificed unblemished lamb: *"When
  the Lord goes through the land to strike
  down the Egyptians, he will see the
  blood on the top and sides of the door-
  frame and will pass over that doorway,
  and he will not permit the destroyer to
  enter your houses and strike you down"*
  (Exod. 12:23).

• The promise is seen in the sacrificial system of Israel. We are guilty sinners worthy of death, but God, in His mercy, provides a way to forgiveness. The true sacrifice is Christ, but this ultimate gift to mankind is foreshadowed in the Old Testament sacrificial system:

> *First he said, "Sacrifices and offerings, burnt offerings and sin offerings you did not desire, nor were you pleased with them"—though they were offered in accordance with the law. Then he said, "Here I am, I have come to do your will." He sets aside the first to establish the second. And by that will we have been made holy through the sacrifice of the body of Jesus Christ once for all (Heb. 10:8-10).*

- The promise is seen in the frequent prophecies that point to a person who will defeat God's enemies and free Israel: *"Strengthen the feeble hands, steady the knees that give way; say to those with fearful hearts, 'Be strong, do not fear; your God will come, he will come with vengeance; with divine retribution he will come to save you'"* (Isa 35:3-4).

- The promise is seen in the vivid descriptions of the earth restored to peace, prosperity, and blessing: *"Then will the eyes of the blind be opened and the ears of the deaf unstopped. Then will the lame leap like a deer, and the mute tongue shut for joy. Water will gush forth in the wilderness and streams in the desert"* (Isa. 35:5-6).

The Old Testament is replete with promises from God that have to do with Him not leaving us to the brokenness, but *instead acting to reverse what sin has done to life and to people.*

45

If you understand this promise of reversing sin to restore life to the way God intended it to be, then you will see why Jesus says what He does when John the Baptist becomes confused about who Jesus is. John is in prison and doesn't hear of Jesus acting like he expected the Messiah to act. He doesn't hear of any great conquest taking place where the enemies are being dealt with. Jesus tells John's disciples, *"Go back and report to John what you hear and see: The blind receive sight, the lame walk, those who have leprosy are cleansed, the deaf hear, the dead are raised, and the good news is proclaimed to the poor"* (Matt. 11:4-5).

What Jesus is saying has to do with what God had been indicating in the Old Testament. There is a great reversal taking place, but that reversal isn't one power now dominating another power; it has to do with reversing what sin has caused. The reversal isn't one of just being forgiven; it is one of being free from the power of sin so that we begin to live the way God made us to live—with humility instead of pride, love instead of hate, others' needs before our own, food for the hungry, and help for those who have little power or few resources. The people of Israel never quite understood what God was promising, but what He was promising was truly something incredible. God was coming to free us from the sin that enslaves us and brings such destruction.

This great rescue and restoration can't be accomplished by anything we do; it can only be accomplished by God Himself. The Old Testament is trying to point us to that fact. We are under a curse, and we can't break it. Worse than that, in our sin, we don't even *want* to break it. We actually want to pursue the things that bring destruction rather than life. We don't need rules that will guide us in what to do—we need a Savior.

47

No More Word from God:

The book of Malachi is the last book of the Old Testament to be written. It ends with God saying this: *"Remember the law of my servant Moses, the decrees and laws I gave him at Horeb for all Israel. See, I will send the prophet Elijah to you before that great and dreadful day of the LORD comes. He will turn the hearts of the parents to their children, and the hearts of the children to their parents; or else I will come and strike the land with total destruction."*

And those are the last words from God we hear. After Malachi, God doesn't speak to His people anymore. That silence lasts for over four hundred years. Think about that—God had spoken to His people through prophets, in dreams, with visions, and in other ways for many years. But now there is silence.

Then, after four hundred years of silence, God speaks again. In the insignificant province of Judah, in the small town of Bethlehem, to two people who were common peasants, in the stall of some animals with a manger as a cradle—a child was born. And the story—God's story, the story He planned from the beginning of creation—is about to be fulfilled. But *that* story is told in another testament.

What you need to know when you read the testament we call "the Old Testament" is its purpose is to prepare you for that greater story, the story of God's arrival to finally "put things right."

We have an amazing God.

————————

Louis Zamperini was a World War II pilot whose plane was shot down over the Pacific Ocean near the enemy, Japan. Zamperini survived adrift in the ocean for forty-seven days. He was captured by the Japanese and spent nearly two and a half years in their prison camp. An Olympic long-distance runner who at one time held the American record in the mile, Zamperini was known for his intense competitive spirit and will. He was a survivor, a fighter who didn't give up. His life story was made into a movie in 2014 based on the book by Laura Hillenbrand, *Unbroken*.

The movie shows Zamperini's spirit being formed in his younger years through his will to compete and win, and through his successes and triumphs. The movie also describes his time in the military. His capture and ill treatment are the dominant focus of the story. As his captors seek to break his spirit, Zamperini develops hatred toward the Japanese, and especially toward one guard in particular. Zamperini survives in spite of incredibly difficult circumstances, and then, freedom comes. The Americans arrive. Japan surrenders. Zamperini and the prisoners return home.

The movie ends with that freedom and home-coming. Zamperini is shown returning to normal life in America. His spirit and will are "unbroken."

The book, though, tells the more accurate story. He did survive all the horrendous adversity that happened to him in that war. However, he did not return to normal life. He was filled with resentment and hatred toward his captors. He became an alcoholic. He lost his job; his marriage disintegrated; he couldn't do anything that required responsibility.

It wasn't until he became "broken" that things would change. His wife became a Christian. She was able to get Zamperini to go to a Billy Graham crusade, where he heard about the God who forgives and makes things new. Zamperini tried to leave the meeting before an altar call was given, but as he was trying to exit, he felt an unexplainable pull to go forward and respond to that invitation. Zamperini gave his life to Jesus Christ that night; he became a child of the living God, and God began a work of restoration, making Zamperini "new."

In being forgiven by God, Zamperini found he could forgive those who had wronged him. His nightmares stopped. He didn't need to escape through alcohol anymore. He broke out of his paralyzing self-loathing and began to find a love for others, including his wife. God repaired his marriage. Zamperini went on a speaking tour to tell others about his life and about what God had done for him. He founded and ran a camp for troubled teenagers. His life now had a great purpose. Louis Zamperini found his freedom, not through the strength of his will to be "unbroken," but through a heart broken enough that he could see and admit his need for a God who loved him.

Others must have realized how incomplete the first movie of *Unbroken* was; a sequel has recently come out, *Unbroken: Path to*

Redemption, that details Zamperini's life after coming home and experiencing the life-changing conversion he had in Christ.

The story of Louis Zamperini is a story of how God comes to rescue and restore a person to the life he was created for. It's the life we begin to experience when we know God as our God. It is the story of what the Bible, Old and New Testaments, is all about.

—PART TWO—

—6—

FOUR HELPFUL BACKSTORIES

In this book, I have given what I believe are the three main storylines of the Old Testament. While there will be much in the Old Testament that will still remain confusing without an understanding of the details—an understanding that requires a study of the culture and context of the book—my contention is that a person who is a committed follower of Jesus Christ can still hear God's primary message in the Old Testament by applying the storylines. These storylines represent God's intention in His singular story of putting things right. It is because of that singular story of redemption that almost everything in the Old Testament relates to some aspect of at least one of these storylines. Those three storylines are these:

- The good life God made becomes broken. Nothing now works right because of this brokenness, including us.

- God's responds to the brokenness. He must act justly and judge the wrong and evil in the world as it deserves, including the evil in us.

- God makes a promise about the brokenness. He is going to overcome brokenness and restore His creation, including us, to what He intended it to be.

There are some books of the Old Testament, however, that will be enhanced greatly and will be considerably less confusing if you know a little more backstory, a little more information about how the book is meant to be read and about its purpose.

I have chosen four books, Job, Ecclesiastes, Daniel, and Esther, for this additional information because I think that without the advanced perspective provided here, each of these four books can be especially confusing or misread. My earlier book, *Help...I Want to Read the Bible but I Don't Know How*, provided such information regarding Psalms and Proverbs; that information won't be duplicated here.

<u>Job:</u>

Job is a book about suffering. More specifically, it is a book about personal suffering. It deals with the question, "Why is this difficulty happening to me when I haven't done anything to deserve it?"

The plot of this story is a simple one.

• God considers Job, a highly successful person with everything a person could want in life, as righteous because of Job's unwavering trust in Him.

- Satan says that Job trusts in God only because of how smoothly Job's life is going. Take away these comforts, says Satan, and Job will turn from his faith.

- God agrees to allow Satan to do his worst to Job, and with that permission, Satan attacks Job with one great calamity after another.

Job's friends all counsel him that these sufferings must have come because of something terrible he has done; otherwise, God would not have permitted these difficulties. Job's friends operate from the viewpoint of "do things right, and you will have blessings in your life; do things wrong, and you will experience sorrows."

Job himself struggles emotionally with why so much suffering has happened to him, but he rejects the idea that difficulties have come specifically because of something he has done to deserve them. Although Job cries out to God, asking why these things have taken place in his life, Job never turns from his ultimate trust in God. You can hear Job's steadfast faith mixed with the confusion and hurt from what is happening to him in his words, "Though he slay me, yet will I hope in him…" (Job 13:15).

God finally appears on the scene to address the situation. He tells Job's friends that Job is right and they are wrong. Job did nothing to deserve these great tragedies in his life. Then God turns to Job to answer the question so many have asked so poignantly throughout history: "Why is this happening to me?"

It is crucial to understand both what God says and what He does not say in responding to this age-old, heart-rending question, or you will simply miss the point of the book altogether. Notice that, in responding to Job, God never actually answers his question of "Why?" Instead, God reminds Job of who He is, highlighting for Job how finite and limited Job is in his understanding of life. In doing so, God is saying to Job, as my Old Testament seminary professor once summarized for me, "Job, it is enough for you to know that I am God and I am good." Rather than giving Job reasons and explanations, God simply points Job to trust in who He is. This trust in the character and purposes of God is what God is always pointing us to, and what Satan is always calling us to doubt.

In this life, rarely are we given the answer to the question, "Why is this happening?" Reasons and explanations cannot ultimately calm the truly hurting heart anyway. The only real response that has the power to help us deal with sorrow lies in trusting in our God—a God who is sovereign, who loves us, and who is good. Even when I can't see or understand His purposes, I will trust in that kind of God!

Ecclesiastes

When you read a mystery book, do you ever turn to the back to find out "who dun it" and then go back to reading the rest of the book? My wife will do that. When I learned about this practice, I was stunned. I went into one of my mini-lectures and vehemently expressed my view that she shouldn't do that. The whole book is ruined if you find out the solution to the book before reading it. I assured her that people simply don't do such a thing.

Then, a few months later, wanting to make some particular point in a sermon I was preaching, I asked my congregation how many of them, in reading a book, have turned to the back in order to know what happens before finishing the book. I had no doubt that very few, if any at all, would raise their hands. But to my great surprise and dismay, I discovered that almost half of my congregation does the same dastardly practice. My wife says that knowing the end helps her relax and she can then enjoy seeing how the author develops the story. I stick by my view: what's the point of reading the rest of the book once you know the solution to the mystery?

Do you do that? Do you read the end of a book before finishing it? I can say only one thing if you do—stop it!

Unless, that is, you are reading the book of Ecclesiastes. Then you should go to the end before reading the rest of the book. If you don't understand the end, you probably aren't going to understand what the book is about.

Ecclesiastes seems like a terribly depressing book (it's the book famous for repeatedly saying, "Meaningless, meaningless; everything is meaningless"). The author of Ecclesiastes is writing about life. He writes about great achievement, popularity, success, religion, wealth, pleasure, friends, family—all the things we typically pursue and desire in making "the good life." His conclusion about every one of these areas is that, even if we pursue them and experience them, in the end, they are meaningless. This "everything is meaningless" conclusion is the reason Ecclesiastes isn't known as a book for great inspirational devotional reading.

However, if we ignore Ecclesiastes, we are greatly short-changing what can be a very thought-provoking and important book. If we give heed to its message, it can protect us from a lot of bad choices in our lives and can be a source of strength and contentment.

The key to reading Ecclesiastes is understanding that Ecclesiastes is a type of "spoof." Ecclesiastes isn't giving us direction on ways to live our life; it is examining what life is like when one tries to live it without God. The conclusion is it doesn't matter what we give ourselves to, how successful or unsuccessful we may be, how much pleasure our experiences give us, or what achievements we may attain. If there is no God, then nothing in life ultimately has real purpose.

Ecclesiastes 12:13, 14 makes the point this way: *"Now all has been heard; here is the conclusion of the matter: Fear God and keep his commandments, for this is the duty of all mankind. For God will bring every deed into judgment, including every hidden thing whether it is good or evil."*

Life is short and temporary; we are but a mist. Such brevity makes everything we do meaningless on its own. Apart from God, life *is* meaningless. Therefore, get connected to the God you were made for, and in serving Him, you will find purpose in everything else (pleasure, success, failure, difficulty, family, friends, etc.). As Christians, we have more understanding than the writer of Ecclesiastes could have had about what happens after we die, so we can make even more sense of why faith in God gives meaning to everything. We live for an eternal kingdom where God will make all things right, and what we do in this life can have eternal significance.

Knowing the end of Ecclesiastes helps you go through and understand exactly what the author is saying about life. The areas he examines are just as relevant, if not more so, today as they were in his day. Ecclesiastes can lead you to examine your own life as well as to discern what is happening in society. Ecclesiastes is a very revealing and insightful book, but you need to read the ending first to see that.

Daniel:

Do you like to discover hidden clues that help you understand or solve something? The book of Daniel has just such a clue. A lot of Bible studies and sermons on Daniel don't seem to recognize this clue as being important, but I believe it provides a crucial key to application in our lives.

The setting: Daniel was written during the time when Israel had been conquered by Babylon and the Jewish people had been taken to Babylon in exile from the promised land God had given to them. The question they were facing, and one that remains enormously relevant to us today, was "How do you remain faithful in living for God when you are surrounded by an entire culture that doesn't care about God and pressures you to compromise what you believe?"

The problem: This book has two very distinct sections that seem to have almost no connection to one another. The first part contains examples of how Daniel and his friends stand steadfastly for God with the implication that we are to do the same (Dan. 1-6). The second half of the book contains prophecies, using highly symbolic imagery, of what is going to happen to the kingdoms of the world in relation to God's kingdom someday in the future (Dan. 7-12). These two sections are so different it's almost as if someone wrote each of them as a separate book and just stuck them together. Do they have any real connection to each other, or is one part just encouraging us to live faithfully and the second part telling us how things end someday in the future?

The clue: I believe the author decidedly wants us to see these two parts of Daniel not as separate writings with different purposes, but as dealing with the exact same theme: living faithfully for God when so much of the culture around you is against the faith you have embraced. The clue is given in the fact that Daniel is written in two different languages — Hebrew and Aramaic. The stories of faithful living in part one start out in Hebrew but then the stories suddenly change to being written in Aramaic. The Aramaic language continues through the end of the stories and carries over for one chapter into the prophecies section. Then suddenly, in chapter eight, the language returns to Hebrew, which hasn't been used since the fourth verse of chapter two.

As Dale Ralph Davis points out in his commentary on Daniel:

> *We should always ask if a writer has left evidence of any design or structure on his work. In this matter I am unable to get around the use of two languages in Daniel: Hebrew in chapter 1, Aramaic roughly chapters 2 – 7, and Hebrew in chapters 8 – 12. Chapter 7 seems the climatic piece of the Aramaic 'stories' section and yet it is not a story but a vision. So language-wise chapter 7 belongs to 2 – 6 and yet category-wise, as a vision, it introduces a series of visions (8 – 12) and itself stands as the first vision in chronological sequence (7:1; 8:1; 9:1 – 2; 10:1). Chapter*

7 then has an overlapping function in the book's structure.[4]

What it means: Many scholarly theories are given as to why two languages are used in the writing of Daniel, but I believe the change in languages is intentional, both by the human author as well as the divine author, who is the One behind it all.

The entire book of Daniel is meant to be a source of strength, encouragement, and courage for God's people who want to live for Him and find that there are many temptations and attacks that will come their way because of this desire. The stories in the first part of the book are written to inspire us. The prophecies of the second part are also meant to inspire our faithful living by reminding us that the only kingdom that really counts in the end is God's kingdom—the eternal one that will be victorious over everything else. The link of the usage of the two languages provides the evidence that the author's intent is for us to see these two sections as a unified theme, not separate and distinct sections.

The message of Daniel is to live for the kingdom that will last forever, not for the things that come and go and that will be judged by the living God. And don't be fooled by the things that oppose the kingdom of God when they appear to be winning, because they aren't. Don't compromise your faith to go along with society; wisely, but steadfastly, stand firm and live faithfully for the kingdom to which you belong.

Daniel is a great book. The prophecies are hard to understand, and you won't be able to understand what is being said without a lot of background information, but the main message is clear: God wins. Stay faithful to the One who wins.

Esther

Do you like irony, humor, and a dramatic turn of events in the stories you read? Then Esther is the book for you. No book in the Bible reads more like a modern-day soap opera than Esther, but Esther has a powerful message and a sense of justice and victory to it.

Esther is one of two books in the Old Testament that don't mention the name of God (the other being the Song of Songs). This fact turns out to be relevant in that it serves to highlight how the providential hand of God is seen everywhere throughout the telling of this dramatic story. The author expects you to see the hand of God behind all the incredible "coincidences" that occur.

The story revolves around four central characters: one, the Persian king Xerxes; two, the villain of the story, Haman; three, the Jewish hero, Mordecai; and four, the heroine, the beautiful niece of Mordecai, Esther. The plot that drives the story is Haman's hatred of the Jews in general, and of Mordecai in particular, that leads him to convince the king to issue an edict that calls for the complete annihilation of the Jews—the genocide of the Jewish people.

In the story of Esther, we find these events:

- Esther rises from her common status to become queen.
- Mordecai foils a plot to have the king killed.
- Esther's position as queen gives her the only opportunity one could have to appeal to the king to rescind the edict.
- The king's inability to sleep leads him to remember just one night before Mordecai was to be hanged by Haman that nothing had been done to honor Mordecai (for previously saving the king's life).

- Esther is received by the king instead of being killed when she comes to him without being summoned.

All of these, and more, are to be seen as God-led events, not simply coincidences.

Instead of Mordecai being hanged on the gallows that Haman had built for him, Haman himself is hanged. King Xerxes responds to Esther's plea for her people, the Jews, by rescinding his edict to have them exterminated.

The book of Esther is fascinating reading. However, we will miss the point of its message and its power to impact our lives if we turn it into simply a book of moral lessons for life such as "see how damaging jealousy can be." The book is telling us of God's sovereign protection of His people. God is in control. God will direct and use events for the accomplishment of His purposes. We can trust in our sovereign God. In the context of God's story, the book of Esther tells us how God saves His chosen people from genocide so that His plan of redemption may continue to take place. The Messiah is to be born from the Jews. God will not let His plan fail. He never does. We can have confidence in the God whose purposes never fail.

SOME CONCLUDING HELPFUL SUGGESTIONS

As you read the Old Testament, here are some things I want to emphasize:

1. There are going to be many things in the Old Testament that you will not understand and may confuse you. Don't worry about it. You are looking for the big picture. The storylines in this book are meant to help you focus on that big picture.

2. There are many times the Old Testament gives direction in how to relate to God, how to treat others, and how to live. These directions and commands serve in two major ways: one, as sign posts as to whether you are in step with God's

kingdom, and two, as a means of highlighting your failure to experience and
express the life for which you were made.
Use them to reflect on your own life in
both those ways and let them help you
draw near to a God of grace whose love
will help you grow in these areas.

3. You will run across books that are par-
ticularly hard and confusing to you. It is
fine to skip them or to skim them. Look
for the areas where you find you can
connect with God's voice. Don't skip
over things too fast though; sometimes
it takes a little reading to be able to catch
the big picture of God's message.

4. A lot of people find it enormously helpful
if they purchase a Life Application Bible
in a translation that reads easily for them.
The benefit of such a Bible is it will have
notes that help explain passages.

5. The Bible isn't meant to be read as simply
an academic exercise. Use your reading

to lead you to reflect on the greatness of God as well as on your own life situation. Christian growth comes from getting to know the heart and character of God and trusting in that God.

One of the quotes I developed for the ministry of Life Impact Connections is, "The gospel is about a restored relationship with God, and it functions on relational dynamics—not principles of self-improvement." When you read the Old Testament, use it to build that relational dynamic with God. Use it to lead you to a sense of awe about your God, to thankfulness, to praise and worship, to confession and godly sorrow, to repentance, and to a deeper trust. Learn who your God is and surrender your heart to Him. Use the Old Testament to interact with God in light of who He is and what He is doing in your life. Do these things, and you will find yourself being encouraged, strengthened, and growing in your faith.

———————————

"The days are coming," declares the Lord, "when I will fulfill the good promise I made to the people of Israel and Judah. In those days and at that time I will make a righteous Branch sprout from David's line; he will do what is just and right in the land. In those days Judah will be saved and Jerusalem will live in safety. This is the name by which it will be called: The Lord Our Righteous Savior."

(Jer. 33:14-16)

—Endnotes—

1. Timothy Keller, *The Prodigal Prophet*, (New York, NY: Viking, an imprint of Penguin Random House LLC, 2018) pp. 10, 11.

2. Timothy Keller, *Generous Justice*, (New York, NY: Dutton, a member of Penguin Group, 2010) p. 4.

3. C. S. Lewis, *The Lion, The Witch and The Wardrobe*, (New York, NY: HarperCollins Publishers, 1994) p. 77.

4. Dale Ralph Davis, *The Message of Daniel*, (Downers Grove, IL: InterVarsity Press, 2013) pp. 22, 23.

—About the Author—

Kent Adrian is pastor of Christ Presbyterian Church in Bradenton, Florida. He is also the founder and president of Life Impact Connections, a Christian speaking and resource ministry seeking to promote healthy Christian discipleship with materials that do not assume significant biblical background or theological understanding on the part of the user. In addition to *YES…The Old Testament CAN Make Sense to You*, Kent has written *HELP…I Want to Read the Bible but I Don't Know How* and *BEDROCK: The Three Qualities of God that Enable You to Handle Life with Strength and Confidence*.

You can learn more about Kent and the ministry of Life Impact Connections by going to *www.lifeimpactconnections.org*.

CPSIA information can be obtained
at www.ICGtesting.com
Printed in the USA
BVHW081431190819
556217BV00025B/2894/P